Mark

Enrichment Magazine

IN THIS ISSUE ...

To the Director

This student folder contains nine study leaflets and the enrichment magazine. Remove the center staple and distribute the leaflets as indicated in the leaders guide. This magazine should be distributed at the first session for use throughout the course.

I0806860

3558 S. Jefferson Ave., St. Louis, MO 63118-3968

1-800-325-3040 • cph.org

Written by Steven Roberge

Edited by Ken Schurb

Cover illustration by Donato Veneziano (14th CE) *The Lion of St. Mark, Symbol of Venice.* © Scala / Art Resource, NY

Graphic design by Christina Ensign

This publication may be available in Braille, in large print, or on cassette tape for the visually impaired. Please allow 8 to 12 weeks for delivery. Write to Lutheran Braille Workers, P.O. Box 5000, Yucaipa, CA 92399; call toll-free 1-800-925-6092; or visit the website: lbwloveworks.org.

Manufactured in the United States of America

3 4 5 6 7 8 9 10 11 12 33 32 31 30 29 28 27 26 25 24

Trialog about the Trinity

The two young Mormon missionaries sat in my living room, saying, "Well . . . of course we are a Christian church." I was outnumbered. With three of us conversing, this was more of a "trialog" than a dialog.

"Allow me to share with you what we believe," the senior of the two continued. "We believe in God, the eternal Father, and in His Son Jesus Christ, and in the Holy Ghost. Our church's name is The Church of Jesus Christ of Latter-day Saints, so you see, we are Christians." Having thus claimed that they were Christians, the two wanted to go on to talk about happy, healthy families. Yet Mormonism's founder, Joseph Smith, taught that the triune God of the Christian faith is not real. If He did exist, Smith asserted, He would be a monstrous God. In fact, though, the triune God is the only true God.

The Many Gods of Mormonism

According to Mormon teaching, there are three gods of whom we know. One god is the Father. Jesus Christ is yet another god. The Holy Ghost is still another. Mormon teaching says that besides these three gods, there are many other gods throughout the universe. This is expressly taught in the Standard Works, the official Mormon Scriptures, in which the gods create the heavens and earth. Like Satan's lie in the Garden of Eden, Mormonism promises members that they can progress to be gods themselves (*Teachings of the Prophet Joseph Smith* [Salt Lake City: Deseret Publishing House, 1979], 346, 369–73).

One, Two, Three

What biblical support do Mormons attempt to use? They often turn to Mark 1:9–11: "Jesus came from Nazareth of Galilee and was baptized by John in the Jordan. And when He came up out of the water, immediately He saw the heavens being torn open and the Spirit descending on Him like a dove. And a voice came from heaven, 'You are My beloved Son.'" There are three gods in this text, Mormons say. My trialog partners told me that the Savior is not a ventriloquist who throws his voice into heaven.

Mormon missionaries are taught to make such statements in an effort to show that Christian teachings are absurd. Upon hearing such things, Christians sometimes become frustrated and angry. Unfortunately, this frustration and anger simply confirm to Mormons that they are right. Mormon missionaries walk away from such angry encounters thinking to themselves, "Oh, well, the world will always hate members of the one true church of Jesus Christ."

It is easy to lose sight of Christ Himself in all the heated debate and emotion. So let's get back to basics.

What Does Jesus Teach?

The word *gods* appears nowhere in Mark 1:9–11. This passage is a narrative. It tells us what happened. The teaching portions of Scripture tell us the meaning of the narrative portions.

Jesus taught that the most important commandment is that "The Lord our God, the Lord is one. . . . Love the Lord your God . . ." Truly, "He is one, and there is no other besides Him" (Mark 12:29–32).

Loving this one true God stands out as of the greatest importance. It is more important than healthy and happy families! Elsewhere in Mark, we find that the genuine family of Christ takes precedence even over biological ties (Mark 3:31–35).

Do Three "Locations" Equal Three Gods?

God is not limited to any one location but is present everywhere at once. This inspires the psalmist to ask,

Where shall I go from Your Spirit?
Or where shall I flee from Your presence?

If I ascend to heaven, You are there!
If I make my bed in Sheol, You are there!
(Psalm 139:7–8)

Through Jeremiah, God says, "Do I not fill heaven and earth?" (Jeremiah 23:24).

The biblical God is present everywhere. He is able to speak from heaven, from the secret places, or even from Sheol if He wishes.

It Makes Sense—or Does It? Does It Have To?

When thinking over some new idea, people often comment on whether it "makes sense." The doctrine of the triune God does not make sense to human reason. We do not understand this God. Does this mean that the teaching must be false, though?

Thank God, He is higher than us (Isaiah 55:8–9). Of course, we do not understand God. He is above heaven (Psalm 148:13). He "looks far down on the heavens" (Psalm 113:6). Thank God! For a god we *could* understand would be a very poor god indeed.

In Matthew 28:19, Jesus said that God's name is "Father . . . Son . . . Holy Spirit," referring to each person of the Godhead. Yet the word *name* in this passage is singular. The psalmist exclaims, "O LORD, our Lord, how majestic is Your name in all the earth!" (Psalm 8:1). God's name tells us something about His inner workings. These workings are not fully known for our consideration, but they are majestic and worthy of our adoration.

Thank God that He reveals Himself. Jesus prayed, "I thank You, Father, Lord of heaven and earth, that You have hidden these things from the wise and understanding and revealed them to little children. . . . All things have been handed over to Me by My Father, and no one knows the Son except the Father, and no one knows the Father except the Son and anyone to whom the Son chooses to reveal Him" (Matthew 11:25, 27).

Misplaced Faith

Misplaced faith in a false god cannot save any more than can misplaced faith in a fake lifeguard. Neither is real. Isaiah wrote of people in his day who were "praying to a god that cannot save." Out of love and concern for His people, God thunders through the prophet Isaiah, "There is no other god besides Me, a righteous God and a Savior" (Isaiah 45:20–21).

The Triune God Embraces Us

Christians do not completely comprehend God (1 Timothy 3:16). Mark recounts that even Jesus' disciples were often clueless about Him and His mission. Like those men, we also are to "grow in the grace and knowledge of our Lord and Savior" (2 Peter 3:18). We also are to "long for the pure spiritual milk" of God's Word (1 Peter 2:2).

Discipleship begins in Baptism. It is no accident that all three persons of the Godhead were invoked at your Baptism. You were baptized into the very name of the God who saves you: "God our Savior . . . by the washing of regeneration and renewal of the Holy Spirit . . . through Jesus Christ our Savior" (Titus 3:4–6). The triune God is the only true God and the God of your salvation.

Don't You Believe in the Ten Commandments?

The caller's voice trembled as she asked her question over live Christian radio. "Sorry, I'm a little nervous . . ." She went on, "My friend asked me, 'Don't you guys believe in the Ten Commandments?' Of course I said, 'Yes!' But then she asked why I work on Saturday and worship on Sunday. She said that the only correct day of worship, according to God, is the seventh-day Sabbath—Saturday! I checked it out in my Bible, and there it was, right in the Ten Commandments!" Like this caller, most Christians worship on Sunday, the first day of the week. Friendly but aggressive Seventh-day Adventists accuse them of teaching the commandments of men as doctrines of God.

Do we not believe in *all* of the Ten Commandments? Yes, we do, but we believe in the seventh-day Sabbath as a commandment that foreshadows something even greater than a day of not working: our salvation in Jesus Christ!

Jesus and the Sabbath

Sunday-worshiping Christians are sometimes stumped when asked about the seventh-day (Saturday) Sabbath: "Remember the Sabbath day, to keep it holy. Six days you shall labor, and do all your work, but the seventh day is a Sabbath to the Lord your God" (Exodus 20:8–10).

The Pharisees questioned Jesus about the Sabbath. "One Sabbath [Jesus] was going through the grainfields, and as they made their way, His disciples began to pick heads of grain. And the Pharisees were saying to Him, 'Look, why are they doing what is not lawful on the Sabbath'?" (Mark 2:23–24).

Jesus responded with an account from the life of King David (see 1 Samuel 21:1–6). David and his friends were hungry, so they ate the bread that was reserved only for the priests. "The Sabbath," Jesus concluded, "was made for man, not man for the Sabbath" (Mark 2:27). The point is clear: human beings are more important than God's ceremonial laws. Christ interpreted God's Law with a method used by the rabbis of his day, *Qal va Chomer*, light and heavy, important and less important. Simply put, if a law applies to a less serious matter, it must apply to a more weighty matter. Standing in this tradition, Christ elsewhere speaks of "the weightier matters of the law" (Matthew 23:23).

The Sabbath was made for man, Jesus declared. "So the Son of Man is lord even of the Sabbath" (Mark 2:28). Jesus the Lord is master over everything, including the Sabbath. He can determine how the Sabbath is used.

Colossian Clarification

Years later, some Christians at Colossae had accepted a hodgepodge of beliefs and practices, including the Sabbath Day, from both pagan and Jewish religions. As a loving corrective, St. Paul wrote them: "See to it that no one takes you captive by philosophy and empty deceit, according to human tradition, according to the elemental spirits of the world, and not according to Christ. For in Him the whole fullness of deity dwells bodily" (Colossians 2:8–9). Christ is superior to both philosophy and tradition. "Therefore let no one pass judgment on you in questions of food and drink, or with regard to a festival or a new moon or a Sabbath. These are a shadow of the things to come, but the substance belongs to Christ" (Colossians 2:16–17). The Sabbath Day was a mere shadow of Christ.

Seventh-day Adventist authors object that in the Greek text of Colossians 2:16 the word *Sabbath* is plural. They say Paul is referring to the many other Sabbaths of the Old Testament, such as Pentecost and Passover. Therefore, they say, the weekly Sabbath Day is still binding on Christians, while these other many Sabbaths were mere shadows of Christ.

However, the Old Testament often groups the seventh-day Sabbath with religious festivals and new moon celebrations (2 Chronicles 2:4; 8:13; Isaiah 1:13; 66:23; Ezekiel 45:17; 46:3; Hosea 2:11), as Paul does in Colossians 2:16. Moreover, the Greek Old Testament often has the seventh-day Sabbath in the plural as "Sabbaths," even in the Sabbath commandment of Exodus 20:8. Paul meant exactly what he seems to mean: the seventh-day Sabbath was a foreshadow of Jesus Christ.

The Lord's Day

Free to worship on any day, Christians began to meet on what they called the Lord's Day. The apostle John had his vision on the Lord's day (see Revelation 1:10). Which day was this?

In AD 110, Ignatius, who had been taught by the apostle John, wrote that Christians no longer observed Sabbaths. Instead, they were meeting on the Lord's Day, the day when Christ rose from the dead. In AD 90, Barnabas wrote a letter declaring that Christians meet on the eighth day, when Christ rose from the dead. Since the seventh day is Saturday, Sunday is both the first day and the eighth day.

© iStockphoto.com / archives

© iStockphoto.com / ilker canikligil

Misusing the Law

We can misuse God's laws to bolster our egos. We look for rules that we find easy to obey, and then we look down our noses on others when they have trouble obeying them. Think of the Sabbath, for instance, where all you have to do is *nothing!*

Using an incident from David's life, Christ demonstrated that people are more important than the Sabbath. On another occasion, He asked, "Is it lawful on the Sabbath to do good or to do harm, to save life or to kill?" (Mark 3:4). Human needs take precedence.

People can also become arrogant over how tolerant and accepting they are. We see this in our culture, just as Paul saw it among the Colossians. They accepted elements of both pagan philosophy and Judaism. Many pluralistic Americans pride themselves on accepting all views. They are intolerant of intolerance. This is false humility (see Colossians 2:18–19).

Private arrogance and secret smugness are sins. We need to repent of our self-righteousness.

Our Sabbath

The Good News is found in the Sabbath as a foreshadowing of Jesus Christ. In union with Him, you rest from the burden of God's Law as well as from all the misuses that people can find for it.

The author of Hebrews held up the Old Testament people and the Sabbath as an example of the rest you now enjoy in Christ (see Hebrews 4:1–10). What do you do to earn your salvation? Nothing! Your salvation in Christ Jesus *is* your Sabbath Day!

© Brand X

Jesus and His Opponents, Then and Now

© iStockphoto.com / Nicole S. Young

As he sat across from me, his intense eyes bore into mine. My Muslim friend and I had had intense religious dialogs before, but this time it was getting heated. I tried not to squirm in my seat as he spoke in a confrontational tone: "Prophet Jesus, the peace and blessings of Allah be upon Him, consistently taught that we attain paradise by obedience to the will of Allah. Just read your own Gospels! It was the apostle Paul who infiltrated the early disciples and taught false doctrines. Only Paul taught salvation by grace alone through faith alone. Also, Prophet Jesus never claimed to be God. He was a mere man, like you or me. Again, it was the false apostle Paul who taught that Jesus was God. Prophet Jesus nowhere teaches these things in the Gospels."

The tone of my friend's voice reminded me of the heated debates between Jesus and His opponents, the scribes and the Pharisees. They, too, took Jesus to be nothing more than a human being, and a deeply misguided one at that. However, in their presence, Jesus spoke and acted as only God can.

Many Opponents, Then and Now

Apparently, some of the scribes and Pharisees mentioned in the Gospels eventually became followers of Jesus, but not completely. Still clinging to notions of works-righteousness, they taught that new Christian converts must all be "circumcised according to the custom of Moses," or they "cannot be saved." They thought it was "necessary . . . to keep the law of Moses" (Acts 15:1–5).

In religious lineage with these pharisaical followers of Jesus stood a later (second century AD) group called the Ebionites, or "the poor ones." This early sect of so-called "Jewish Christians" was actually known for its rejection of basic Christian teachings, such as the divine nature of Jesus Christ, the Trinity, and Paul's teaching of salvation by God's grace through faith in Christ. Notably, as some Muslims defend their religion in writing and public debate today, they claim the Ebionites as spiritual ancestors (e.g., Muslim apologist M. A. Yussef, *The Dead Sea Scrolls, the Gospel of Barnabas and the New Testament* [Indianapolis: American Trust Publications, 1990], 59–65). In fact, falsehoods about Jesus taught by Islam today resemble those held by several heretical groups from the Church's early history (C. George Fry, "The Quranic Christ," *Concordia Theological Quarterly* 43, no. 3 [June 1979], 207–21 [also at www.ctsfw.edu/library/files/pb/1655]).

As Jesus spoke in the Gospels to the scribes and Pharisees of His day, so He continued to speak through the Gospels to His opponents of the second century and the centuries since. He speaks to our Muslim friends today, as of course He speaks to His Church.

Jesus Forgives

In Mark 2:1–12, Jesus was surrounded by His fellow Jews. When a paralytic was brought before Him, He said, "Son, your sins are forgiven" (Mark 2:5). The man had done nothing to deserve this grace. Jesus' declaration might have even come as a surprise to him and his friends; they had come for healing.

Bystanders reacted strongly against Jesus' words of forgiveness. "Some of the scribes were sitting there, questioning in their hearts, 'Why does this man speak like that? He is blaspheming! Who can forgive sins but God alone?' "(Mark 2:6–7).

These scribes were absolutely correct. Only God can forgive sins. "Against You, You only have I sinned," King David prayed to the Lord (Psalm 51:4). Christ was indeed acting as God, who spoke through the prophet Isaiah: "I, I am He who blots out your transgressions for My own sake, and I will not remember your sins. . . . Turn to Me and be saved, all the ends of the earth! For I am God, and there is no other" (Isaiah 43:25; 45:22).

Jesus Heals

Jesus did not tell the objectors that they would have to accept His teachings blindly. Rather, He graciously showed that He had power behind His words: " 'That you may know that the Son of Man has authority on earth to forgive sins'—He said to the paralytic— 'I say to you, rise, pick up your bed, and go home.' And he rose and immediately picked up his bed and went out before them all, so that they were all amazed and glorified God, saying, 'We never saw anything like this!' " (Mark 2:10–12).

Only God has authority to forgive sins. Only God has the power to heal as Jesus did. Through Moses, the Lord had said, "See now that I, even I, am He, and there is no god beside Me; I kill and I make alive; I wound and I heal; and there is none that can deliver out of My hand" (Deuteronomy 32:39).

Christ demonstrated His divine authority. Only God heals. Only God forgives.

Denying Who

Distrust or lack of faith causes estrangement and separation to any relationship. It brings about a *break* in that relationship. So here: when a person does not take Jesus at His word, but rather rejects His word, such a person separates himself or herself from Jesus and His gifts. Tragically, when people distrust Jesus, do not believe Him—indeed, reject *who* Jesus is—they place themselves outside His gifts and graces. Therefore, Jesus said, "Unless you believe that I am He you will die in your sins" (John 8:24).

Denying What

To distrust and disbelieve *what* Jesus has done for us also causes a break in the relationship. In the person of Christ, God Himself came and died to get us into heaven. Jesus said that "the Son of Man came . . . to give His life as a ransom for many" (Mark 10:45).

People who deny that Christ's life and death were sufficient will try to obtain forgiveness some other way. It might be circumcision, obedience to the will of God, or even Christian living. The Bible declares emphatically that such a person has been "severed from Christ" and has "fallen away from grace" (Galatians 5:4). Paradoxically, trying to obtain salvation by works does not save at all. It damns. It shows distrust and unbelief in the sufficiency of Christ's ransom.

Christ's Voice Today

Matthew's Gospel has an account parallel to Mark 2:1–12. This section in Matthew concludes, "When the crowds saw it, they were afraid, and they glorified God, who *had given such authority to men*" (9:8, emphasis added). Jesus gave the power to forgive sins to His believing people, the Christian Church (see Matthew 16:19; 18:18–20; John 20:23). Christian pastors exercise this authority as public "stewards of the mysteries of God" (1 Corinthians 4:1). We need never doubt that the Absolution is the living voice of Jesus, God Himself: "Your sins are forgiven." When *He* forgives sins, they *are* forgiven!

RED-LETTER CHRISTIANS

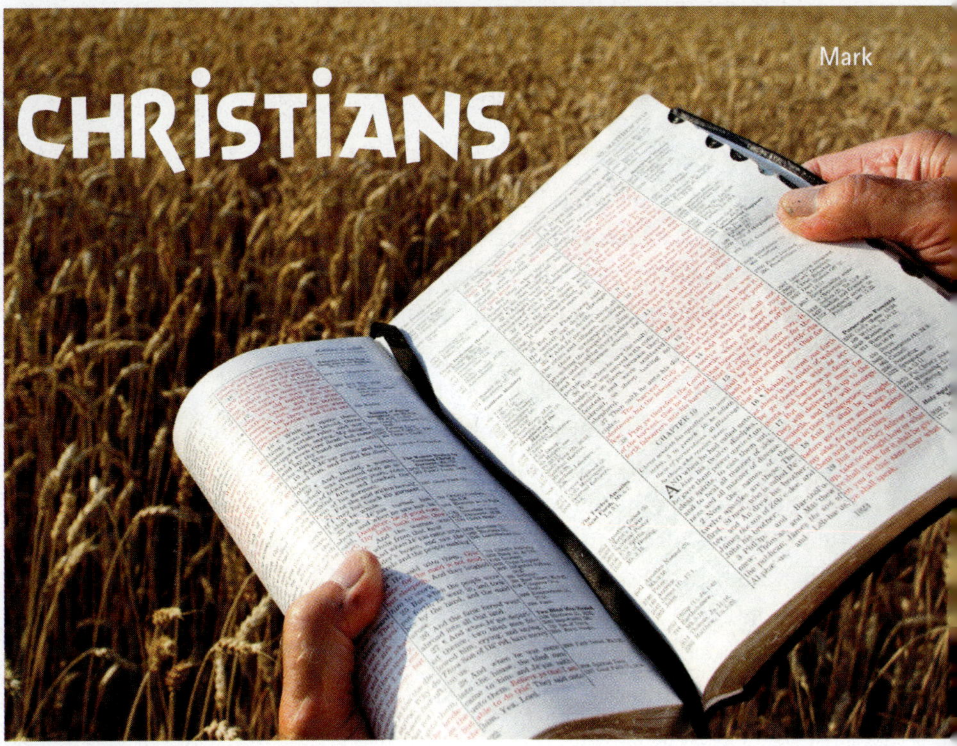

There is an interesting group of people whom we might call "Red-Letter Christians." In many editions of the New Testament, Christ's words are printed in red. A red-letter Christian places the words in red—the teachings of Christ in the Gospels—above the rest of the Bible. According to red-letter Christians, these words in red encompass our primary concerns: the poor, the environment, war, improving education, and care for those who suffer due to sexual orientation, gender, or race. The red words call us away from consumerist greed, urging us to be merciful to others. Red-letter Christians also allege that Christ is silent on the issues of gun control, homosexuality, and abortion, so these should not be the primary concerns of Christians.

One political candidate, when asked about his position on gay marriage, referred his listeners to the Sermon on the Mount, saying it is "more central than an obscure passage in Romans." (He was probably thinking of Romans 1, where St. Paul explicitly condemns homosexual and lesbian behaviors.) Seeing the Sermon on the Mount as central may be attractive. It's simple; it may also be attractive for political correctness. But should Christians, in fact, cling to the words in red while downplaying, trivializing, and even dismissing the rest of Scripture?

Certainly, the words in red address social concerns and embody many of Christ's teachings about love. The word used for love in the Greek of the Gospels is almost always *agape*: commitment to do whatever is best for the other person, regardless of feelings. See, for example, Christ's command to have love even toward enemies (Matthew 5:43–47).

The Words in Red Bless the Words in Black

What does Christ teach about His apostles and their words? First, He chose twelve men to be His immediate disciples (Matthew 9:9; 10:2–4; Mark 3:16–19; Luke 5:27; 6:12–16; John 1:35–51; 17:6). He later commissioned them to teach as His official spokesmen (Matthew 28:18–20; John 20:21; Acts 1:8). The teachings of these twelve were inspired by the Holy Spirit (John 14:26; 15:26–27; 16:13–15).

When Christ sent out the twelve to preach in His name, He said: "If any place will not receive you and they will not listen to you, when you leave, shake off the dust that is on your feet as a testimony against them" (Mark 6:11). The apostles' message was so important that those who rejected it would incur this symbolic testimony against them.

Christ also appointed seventy-two disciples, saying, "The one who hears you hears Me, and the one who rejects you rejects Me, and the one who rejects Me rejects Him who sent Me" (Luke 10:16). To accept the words of Christ's appointed spokesmen is to accept Christ's own Word.

Christ appointed another apostle, Paul (Acts 9:1–6). All of the apostles and their writings are the authoritative words of God Himself. With His words in red, Christ blesses the words in black with divine authority.

All Scripture has His stamp of approval. The better way to think of being a red-letter Christian, then, is to *start* with the words in red, but then to take in all of God's Word. Are you a red-letter Christian? Super! Keep reading!

© iStockphoto.com / Chris Schmidt

Silence of the Lamb?

Admittedly, gun control, homosexuality, and abortion are not directly addressed in any words we have from Christ Himself. However, as faithful sheep, we want to listen to our Shepherd's voice as closely as possible. What can we legitimately infer about these issues from the words in red?

First, Christ saw no reason why His people could not own weapons, at least when dangerous transgressors were about. He cited a prophecy from Isaiah 53 that He would be "numbered with the transgressors" (Luke 22:37). Knowing that His disciples would be in danger, He said, " 'Let the one who has no sword sell his cloak and buy one.' . . . And they said, 'Look, Lord, here are two swords.' And He said to them, 'It is enough' " (Luke 22:36–38).

Is Christ completely silent on homosexuality? "What comes out of a person is what defiles him. For from within, out of the heart of man, come evil thoughts, sexual immorality, theft, murder, adultery, coveting, wickedness, deceit, sensuality, envy, slander, pride, foolishness. All these evil things come from within, and they defile a person" (Mark 7:20–23). In the Greek text of Mark, the word *porneia* (translated here as "sexual immorality") encompasses all sexual sins, including homosexual behavior. Jesus' own Bible, the Old Testament, defines these sexual sins in Leviticus 18:22. To ignore homosexuality is to ignore the Bible that Jesus held dear. (*Porneia* is not the only sin that defiles, however. It would amount to deceit, which is also condemned by Jesus, to pretend that homosexuality is somehow "worse" than other sins.)

© iStockphoto.com / Sheryl Griffin

What about abortion? Let's start again with the words in red. Christ constantly quoted the Old Testament as authoritative (Mark 14:27), distinguishing this Word of God from mere human tradition (Mark 7:11–13). Christ points out that the Holy Spirit inspired the Old Testament (Mark 12:36). He cited as Scripture its three traditional divisions: the Torah (Mark 7:10); the Prophets (Mark 7:6); and the Writings (Mark 12:10–11).

Both Jesus and the Old Testament make it clear that murder is sin (Mark 7:21; Exodus 20:13). Further, the same Old Testament shows the value of human life from the moment of conception. King David traced his personal history: "In sin did my mother conceive me" (Psalm 51:5). Thus, David was himself ("me") at the moment of conception, a viable and valuable human life.

The Words in Red: More Than Just Social Issues

Abusing the poor, abortion, greed, homosexuality, racism, even rejecting the words in black—all these sins defile us. Yet Jesus Christ is more than a man who stands against these sins or against social injustice. He is the Son of God (Mark 1:1, 11; 3:11; 5:7; 9:7; 13:32; 15:39). Like any son, He has the same nature as His Father. (See Mark 12:1–11.)

Like His Father, He has done the impossible. When He observed, "It is easier for a camel to go through the eye of a needle than for a rich person to enter the kingdom of God," the disciples wondered, 'Then who can be saved?' Jesus replied, 'With man it is impossible, but not with God. For all things are possible with God'" (Mark 10:25–27).

The Bible's central message, red and black words alike, is "to make you wise for salvation through faith in Christ Jesus" (2 Timothy 3:15). "You search the Scriptures," Jesus said, "because you think that in them you have eternal life; and it is they that bear witness about Me" (John 5:39).

A Taste of Heaven

Jesus Christ was wrong! He predicted that He would return and establish His kingdom within His disciples' lifetime. Then He was crucified. The disciples died off one by one. Jesus never returned. That makes Him a false prophet. All of this is a claim from Bertrand Russell's infamous book *Why I Am Not a Christian*. Such gripping claims are also typical of modern atheist and agnostic celebrities such as Christopher Hitchens and Richard Dawkins. Twenty-first-century Christians are barraged by many such hostile jibes. Their faith is belittled on television and in print media. Scripture shows these jibes to be paper tigers.

Then what did Christ mean when He said, "Truly, I say to you, there are some standing here who will not taste death until they see the kingdom of God after it has come with power" (Mark 9:1)? Jesus meant just what He said, that the disciples would not die until they saw the kingdom of God.

Out of Context

Who likes to be taken out of context? No one, it seems, is taken out of context more than Jesus Christ. Russell misquoted Matthew's Gospel, omitting some important words: "Truly, I say to you, there are some standing here who will not taste death until *they see* the Son of Man coming in His kingdom" (Matthew 16:28). The parallel verses in Luke 9:27 and Mark 9:1 say "until *they see* the kingdom of God" (all emphases added). Rather than the actual second coming, Christ foretold *a vision* of Him and His kingdom with the word *see*.

A Vision of Heaven

Six days after Christ spoke about seeing God's kingdom, He took Peter, James, and John up a "high mountain by themselves" (Mark 9:2). There, they saw what Jesus promised. "And He was transfigured before them, and

His clothes became radiant, intensely white, as no one on earth could bleach them. And there appeared to them Elijah with Moses" (Mark 9:2–4). The phrase "as no one on earth" and the presence of Moses and Elijah convey that it was a heavenly vision.

Moses and Elijah appear in glory, which will be our heavenly state, revealing our transfigured glory. Moses died (Deuteronomy 34). Elijah was taken alive into heaven (2 Kings 2:11–12). In the same way, many have entered Christ's heavenly kingdom by death, and some will enter it alive at the end of time (1 Thessalonians 4:17).

Peter, James, and John recognized Moses and Elijah, although these prophets lived centuries earlier. Paul reminded the Christians in Corinth that once they see Christ face-to-face, they will "know fully" (1 Corinthians 13:12). In heaven, God's people will exist in perfect relationships, even though they were separated by thousands of years of time in this world.

Notice, too, the presence of the Son in Mark 9:2–3. We hear the Father's voice in verse 7: "This is My beloved Son; listen to Him." Why doesn't Mark mention the Holy Spirit? Here may be a reason: when the Israelites left Egypt, the Lord went ahead of His people in a thick cloud. Through the night, He went ahead of them in a flaming fire (Exodus 13:21–22). Later, the prophet Isaiah commented on the exodus narrative and suggested that the cloud was the Holy Spirit Himself (Isaiah 63:11–14). At the transfiguration, there was a cloud that "overshadowed" Jesus and His disciples (Mark 9:7). This event was not unlike heaven, which is blessed with the fullness of the triune God's presence. Mark 9 pictures a foretaste of heaven.

Hell

The Gospel according to Mark contains no corresponding vision of hell. There are descriptions of it, though. Out of love and concern for people, Jesus warned of hell as "unquenchable fire . . . where their worm does not die and the fire is not quenched" (Mark 9:44, 48). Worse, Jesus leaves us no excuses to cover our guilt: "If your hand causes you to sin, cut it off. It is better for you to enter life crippled than with two hands to go to hell, to the unquenchable fire. And if your foot causes you to sin, cut it off. It is better for you to enter life lame than with two feet to be thrown into hell. And if your eye causes you to sin, tear it out" (Mark 9:43–47).

"If your foot causes you to sin, cut it off." In other words, whatever is causing you to sin, get rid of it! Of course, our body parts do not cause us to sin. Our hearts cause us to sin. Jesus said so in Matthew 5:27–30, where He indicates that the source of sin is not our eyes or our hands, but our heart. Through repentance, you need to be cut off from your sinful self.

Your Inheritance, the Kingdom Prepared for You

Some Christians turn to the Book of Revelation, especially its final chapter, to find a literal description of Christ's heavenly kingdom. Careful, though! The very beginning of the book says: "The revelation of Jesus Christ, which God gave Him to show to His servants the things that must soon take place. He made it known by sending His angel to His servant John" (1:1). The original Greek word for "make it known" stands out as important here. It means to "express with signs," or as we would usually say in English, "to signify." The Book of Revelation, then, is a book of *signs*, and signs need to be read as the figures of speech that they are.

Mark 9 shows that God's kingdom is primarily about relationships with the triune God of love and with fellow believers. After all, Scripture often describes God's kingdom as our inheritance (Matthew 25:34; 1 Corinthians 6:9–11; 15:50, etc.), and inheritance goes to those who have a relationship as family or close friends. As Jesus said, Christians are His brothers and sisters and mothers (Mark 3:31–35). Those who are members of His family inherit the Kingdom seen by the disciples at the transfiguration.

Your relationship with the Father and the Son (and the Holy Spirit) is the only "thing" you will carry with you into the life to come. But what a relationship! John, one of the eyewitnesses of the transfiguration, put it this way: "Our fellowship is with the Father and with His Son Jesus Christ. And we are writing these things so that our joy may be complete" (1 John 1:3–4).

Avoid Sects and Falsehoods

When I first converted to the Lutheran Church, my girlfriend was surprised. Yet I was even more surprised at her reaction. "You can follow Martin Luther if you want. As for me, I will serve Jesus! I do not follow the doctrines of mere humans like this man Luther. I am simply a Christian. I just believe in the Bible. I only follow Jesus Christ. When I read the New Testament, I do not see 'Lutheran' there. I see only the name 'Christian.' "

Has this ever happened to you? Admittedly, phrases such "Jesus only" and "no doctrines of mere men" ring true in the back of every Christian mind. Simply liking Luther or disliking other Christians is no reason to be Lutheran. The only reason to be Lutheran is because being Lutheran is to be truly biblical and Christ-centered. In other words, it is important to avoid both sects and falsehoods.

Sects

John reported to Jesus about a man who was driving out demons "in Your name. We tried to stop him," John explained, "because he was not following us" (Mark 9:38–41). The phrase "in Your name" means much more than the mere verbal mention of the syllables "Je-sus." In biblical thinking, a person's name stands for the person himself. Phrases such as "in the name of Jesus Christ" mean "in union with the person of Jesus Christ." Whoever this otherwise unidentified man may have been, he was a genuine follower of Christ—a true Christian casting out demons in union with Christ.

Nonetheless, John wanted to stop him because he was not one of Jesus' regular disciples. Jesus responded in no uncertain terms: "Do not stop him, for no one who does a mighty work in My name will be able soon afterward to speak evil of Me" (Mark 9:39). There was no good reason for John to hinder this man. What John was practicing was sectarianism. He was causing needless division.

Some years later, the apostle Paul wrote to the Church of Corinth: "There is quarreling among you, my brothers. What I mean is that each one of you says, 'I follow Paul,' or 'I follow Apollos,' or 'I follow Cephas,' or 'I follow Christ.' Is Christ divided?" (1 Corinthians 1:11–13). Christ and His Body are one, and we are His Body (1 Corinthians 12). Instead of acting like the Corinthians, we need to be patient when we step on one another's toes in our Church life. In such situations, as Jesus said, "The one who is not against us is for us" (Mark 9:40).

Dividing Christians unnecessarily is sinful, even if it is done in the name of Christ. That would be the sin of sectarianism.

Falsehoods

So why are there different church bodies? Is this biblical? Shouldn't all people who call themselves Christian simply meet in some huge building and worship as one? Is there ever a legitimate reason for one church to divide from another?

Paul at length wrote the Corinthians that *"there must be* factions among you in order that those who are genuine among you may be recognized" (1 Corinthians 11:19, emphasis added). Divisions draw the lines of demarcation clearly, so that a group that confesses genuine biblical faith stands out as easier to recognize. As deplorable as division is, sometimes it comes as a necessary last resort when the teaching of God's Word is at stake. People in the Church at Corinth were behaving rudely toward one another during the Lord's Supper (1 Corinthians 11:20–21). Worse, they were not examining themselves before they ate (11:28). In this Holy Meal, Christ's body is present in and with the bread (10:16–17), yet they did not recognize His body (11:29). It never should have come to this, but on several subjects the Corinthians had deep doctrinal divisions among themselves. If they had pretended to be one unified church, it would have been a lie. That would have been the sin of unionism.

Patient as we need to be with one another's faults and foibles, Christ calls us to be downright impatient with anything that gets in the way of people hearing God's Word and taking it with the utmost seriousness: "Whoever causes one of these little ones who believe in Me to sin, it would be better for him if a great millstone were hung around his neck and he were thrown into the sea" (Mark 9:42). False doctrine never helps matters in the Church. When God's Word is set aside, contaminated, or drained of its comfort, things turn unsafe for poor sinners. In this situation, whoever is not with Christ is against Him.

"Salt is good, but if the salt has lost its saltiness, how will you make it salty again?" (Mark 9:50). If unsalty salt is unthinkable, so is having God's Word but not humbly hearing it.

Listen to the Word

When the disciples were arguing among themselves about who was the greatest, Mark reports that Jesus "sat down and called the twelve. And He said . . ." (Mark 9:34–35). The path to unity of belief is to listen to our Master's words.

We not only listen to the words of our Master, Jesus, but we also listen to the words of His chosen spokesmen, the apostles. For example, at the Acts 15 Jerusalem council, Christians listened to the apostles' teachings. Where the apostles' teachings are, the Holy Spirit is also there to guide and instruct. Their teachings are in our sacred library, the New Testament.

Back to the Gospel

Jesus told His disciples what was going to happen: "The Son of Man is going to be delivered into the hands of men, and they will kill Him. And when He is killed, after three days He will rise" (Mark 9:31). The death and resurrection of Jesus Christ is the heart of the Gospel. The proclamation of this message is always what suffers when there is sectarianism and false teaching. We need to avoid both for the sake of all people, for whom Christ died, including us.

At the same time, this Good News is what will keep us out of false teaching and sectarianism. The grace of God in all its sweetness draws you close to Him and makes you patient with others.

So, Why Do You Baptize Babies?

"So, why do you guys baptize babies?" Christians who do so are sometimes stumped by this question. Some Christians maintain that babies should be excluded from Baptism because they can't yet believe. Babies, they say, are unable to repent or to make a decision to receive Jesus Christ as their personal Lord and Savior. Baby baptizers are told that they ignorantly follow tradition when they baptize infants, and they would not do so if they knew their Bibles better.

What about all this? Are there passages in the Bible that teach infant Baptism? Indeed there are, even though they do not use the term "infant Baptism." Look carefully at the biblical text. In Scripture, God clearly teaches the Church to baptize babies.

Look Carefully

Consider for a moment the inclusion of women in the Lord's Supper. No Church in principle specifically denies the Lord's Supper to women.

Yet is there a *direct* command to include women in the Lord's Supper? In the Upper Room on that first Maundy Thursday, when Christ said, "Do this," He was, after all, speaking directly to an all-male group of disciples.

Is there an *explicit* example of women partaking of the Lord's Supper anywhere in the New Testament? Read through the Gospels, the Acts of the Apostles, and various epistles. You will find no specific mention of women eating and drinking the Lord's Supper.

So why include women? Scripture implies that they be included. Women are members of the Church no less than men, and the Church partakes of the Lord's Supper (1 Corinthians 11:17–34). So we gladly include women in this joyous Sacrament.

In a similar way, there is no direct biblical command to "baptize infants" and no specific scriptural example of them being baptized. Yet the inclusion of babies in Baptism is repeatedly implied by God in His Word.

In Mark 10:13–16, people were bringing children to Jesus that He might touch them and bless them. Luke 18:15–17 recounts this very scene, noting that these were actually "infants," babies in arms. Thus, people were bringing to Jesus infants not yet old enough, as people today might put it, to understand what was going on.

The disciples tried to stop this, perhaps mistakenly thinking that babies were not old enough for Christ's attention or blessing. "When Jesus saw it," Mark reports, "He was indignant and said to them, 'Let the children come to Me; do not hinder them, for to such belongs the kingdom of God' " (Mark 10:14).

The "back story" to this scene took place about two thousand years earlier, when God gave Abraham His covenant. Eight-day-old infants were to be circumcised and included in this covenant. One who was not circumcised was "cut off from his people" (Genesis 17:14). Now think again about Jesus in Mark 10. Rather than being "cut off" from God's people, He said of the infants who were brought to Him that the kingdom of God belongs to such as these.

Jesus continued, "I say to you, whoever does not *receive* the kingdom of God like a child shall not enter it" (Mark 10:15, emphasis added). Infants do not have the kingdom of God by right. Jesus did not say that the kingdom of God belongs to any and all infants; He said it belongs to the infants brought to Him, those infants who "receive" it. Jesus held up the infants as examples of those who receive God's kingdom at whatever age. Helpless children receiving Christ by faith become the model for all Christian conversion.

How do infants receive God's kingdom today? How are they brought to Jesus? In Baptism! "Christ loved the church and gave Himself up for Her, so that He might sanctify her, having cleansed her by the washing of water with the word, so that He might present the church to Himself in splendor" (Ephesians 5:25–26).

Faith: Relational, Not Rational

"Belief," "faith," and "trust" are relational terms in the Bible. God engenders loving trust even in the hearts of infants: "You made me trust You at my mother's breasts" (Psalm 22:9). God's kingdom extends to nursing infants. Although they cannot pronounce the word "faith," God enables them to trust.

Jesus quoted Psalm 8, "Out of the mouth of infants and nursing babies You have prepared praise" (Matthew 21:16). Some may think that a baby cannot have faith in God because they figure that faith is essentially knowledge. Yet in Scripture, faith is essentially trust and receiving the blessings of Christ.

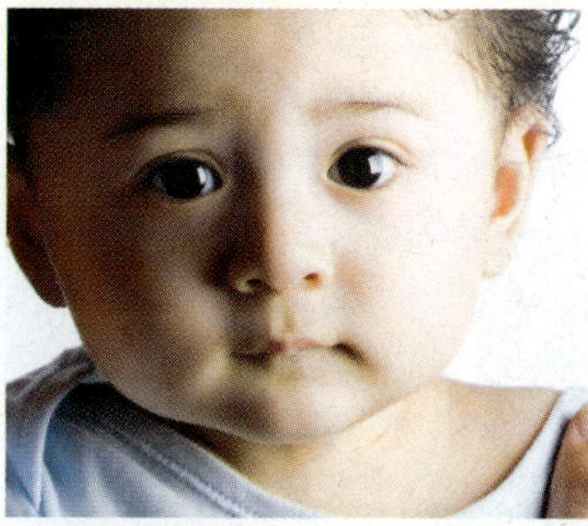

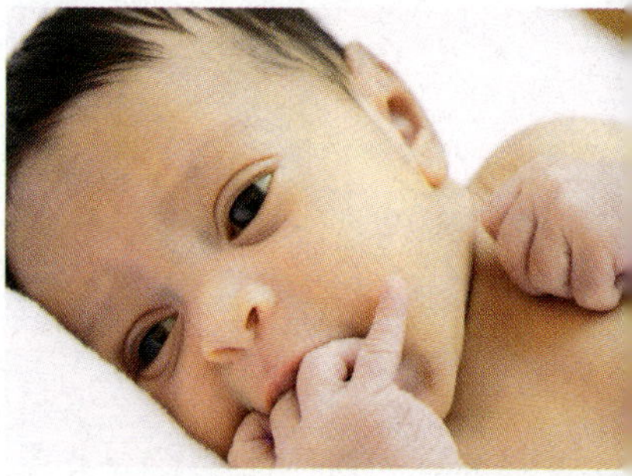

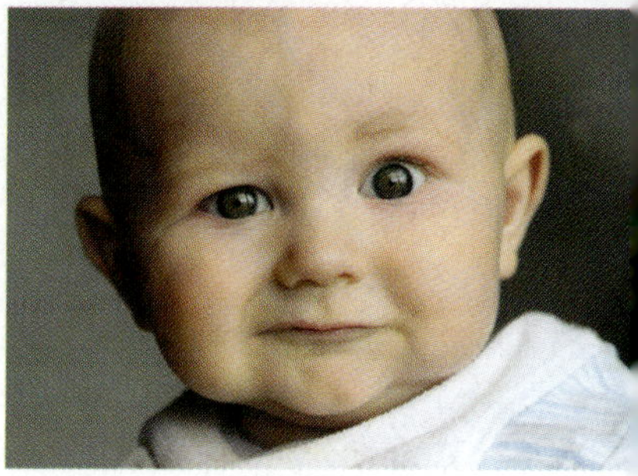

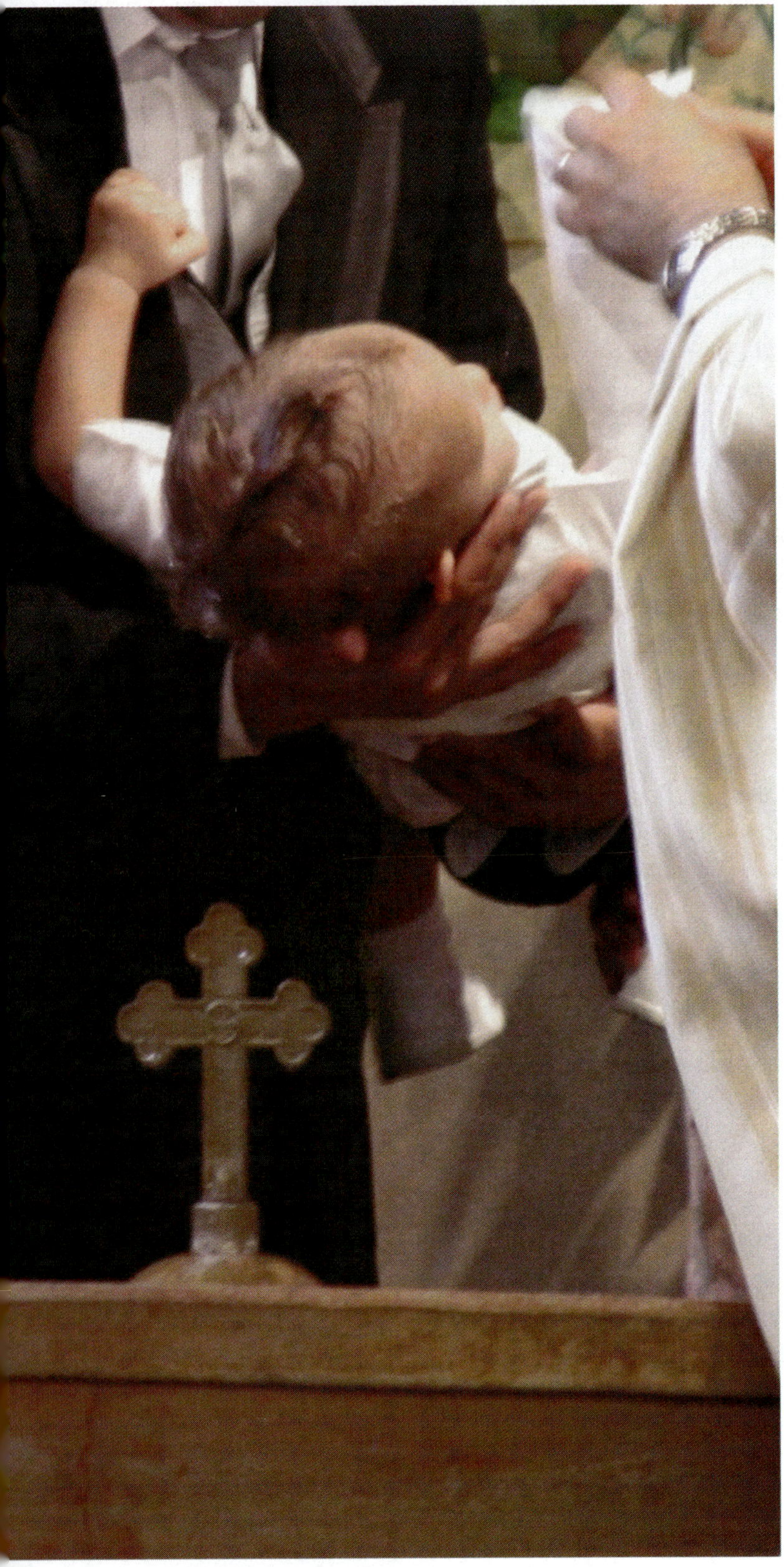

Digging Deeper

The New Testament does two things with circumcision. First, it replaces circumcision with Baptism. Baptism *is* the Christian's circumcision (Colossians 2:11–12). Second, the New Testament universalizes this "new circumcision" and imparts it to both males and females (Galatians 3:27–28). Baptism is therefore given to males and females, to new converts and babies.

Peter said, "Repent and be baptized every one of you in the name of Jesus Christ for the forgiveness of your sins, and you will receive the gift of the Holy Spirit. For the promise is for you and for your children" (Acts 2:38–39). If you had been standing in the crowd listening to Peter, you might have never heard of Christian Baptism. You would not have heard anyone ask, "Why do you baptize babies?" What would you have thought when Peter said, "The promise is for you and for your children"? Would you have thought, "It is for me now, and it will be for my children when they are old enough to understand"? Or would you have taken the words "The promise is for you and your children" to mean just what they said?

The Promise Is for You and Your Children

Do not undervalue Baptism—for yourself or for anyone else! Scripture *promises* that the Holy Spirit is present in Baptism, even for the infant.

Are you single? Are you without children? What Peter said applies to you. "The promise is *for you!*" Do you have kids? Pay attention to what Peter said: "The promise is . . . *for your children*." Jesus Christ wants a relationship with you *and* with your baby.

In Mark 10, Jesus took babies in His arms. He "blessed them, laying His hands on them" (v. 16). To such as these, to such babies as are brought to Jesus, the kingdom of God belongs.

How do you bring a baby to Jesus? The Lord Himself said, "Go therefore and make disciples of all nations, baptizing them in the name of the Father and of the Son and of the Holy Spirit" (Matthew 28:19).

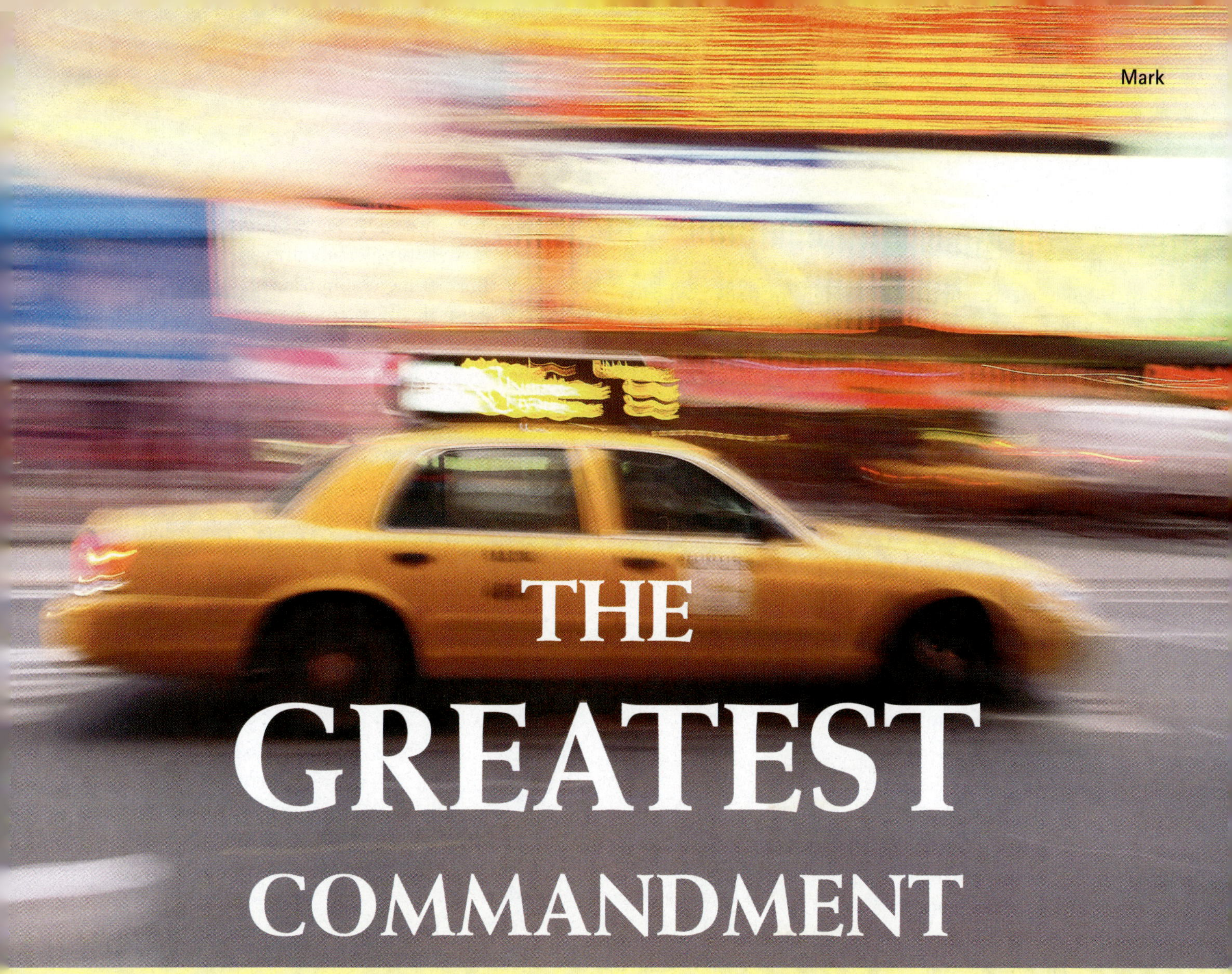

THE GREATEST COMMANDMENT

(*Based on Mark* 12:28–34)

A recent news report said that certain taxicab drivers were refusing to transport blind people who had guide dogs. Why? The drivers' religion teaches that dogs are unclean. They said they would rather obey God than get near a dog, even to transport a blind person in a taxi. You may find this story outrageous, even cruel. Perhaps you feel this way because Christ's ethical teachings have influenced your thinking. These ethical teachings have lost none of their importance.

Christians should emphasize the *central* teaching in Scripture: salvation by grace alone through faith alone in Jesus Christ alone. Will we lose sight of this cardinal teaching if we consider biblical ethics? Actually, biblical ethics go hand-in-hand with God's grace, and they are impossible without it.

Ethically Speaking

In Mark 12, one of the scribes overheard Christ disputing with His opponents. He had a question for Jesus: "Which commandment is the most important of all?" (v. 28). The scribe was asking a question often discussed by the rabbis, the legal question of "heavy and light." The rabbis recognized that some parts of God's law are heavy and important, while other parts are light and less important. Christ Himself elsewhere spoke of "the weightier matters of the law" (Matthew 23:23). On yet another occasion, He quoted the prophet Hosea, "I desire mercy, and not sacrifice" (Matthew 12:7).

In answer to the questioning scribe, Jesus spoke of the "most important" commandment: "Hear, O Israel: The Lord our God, the Lord is one. And you shall love the Lord your God with all your heart and with all your soul and with all your mind and with all your strength" (Mark 12:29–30, quoting Deuteronomy 6:4–5). Monotheism, the worship of one God, stands at the center of Jesus' teachings. It forms the starting point for His ethics. There is only one God. From Him all commandments flow. We are to love Him first and with everything we have.

Christ's answer up to this point may have seemed redundant. The scribe could have been thinking to himself, "Yes, we are to put God *first.* That's the whole reason I am asking this question: Which commandment *of God* is most important?"

St. Augustine once said, "Love God, then do as you please." For if we love God, we will naturally wish to seek out His will and obey Him. So the question naturally follows: once we value God above all else, what does He want us to do? Again quoting the Old Testament, Christ continued: "You shall love your neighbor as yourself" (Mark 12:31).

Too often, we make this second command suffer by comparison with the first. We play one command against the other as an excuse to treat others poorly. Think of those taxi drivers who put obedience to God above compassion toward people.

Yet Jesus said, "There is no other commandment greater than these" (Mark 12:31). He saw *both* of them as important. Since it is *God* who commands us to love our neighbors, loving them is as important as loving Him.

As a matter of fact, to love our neighbors is really to show love toward God. "Whoever receives one such child in My name receives Me," Jesus said, "and whoever receives Me, receives not Me but Him who sent Me" (Mark 9:37). On the day of judgment, Jesus will say, "As you did it to one of the least of these My brothers, you did it to Me" (Matthew 25:40). Christians cannot use God as an excuse to treat other people poorly.

A Question of Motive

So far, we have been examining the basic ethic of Jesus: Love God. Love your neighbor. But why? Why love God?

Consider various motives for being an ethical person. The first is fear of hell: I love others because the threat of eternal torment hangs over my head. The second motivation is fear of earthly punishment in this life: if I do not love, then God may curse my finances, destroy my family, or take everything away from me, like He did to Job. The third motivation for loving is fear of guilt: if I do not love, then my conscience will nag me. All of these motivations obviously have their roots in fear. The world is full of fear-based religions.

Some of these motives can be found in the Bible, but none of them stands out as Christians' primary motivation for loving God and neighbor. Why do we love, then? What is the *primary* biblical motivation for loving?

Think of St. Paul's letter to a church he had not yet visited, the church at Rome. To prepare for spending time with the people of this church, Paul wrote them a point-by-point presentation of the Christian faith, the Epistle to the Romans. When he finally arrived, he and they would literally be on the same page.

Law

Paul outlined what has been called "the Roman road" as he presented the Christian faith in this letter. His first big point was that all people are sinners, Jew and Gentile alike. No amount of ethical behavior is enough, and what we sinners do will never be good enough to please God! All people have a desperate need to be righteous before Him (Romans 1:18–3:20).

Gospel

Second, Paul wrote that God Himself has provided a way for us to be righteous. He sent His Son, Jesus Christ, to take our punishment upon Himself. God's justice has been satisfied. We are, therefore, off the hook, freed from the prospect of God's punishment. God has *declared* us righteous (Romans 3:21–26).

At length, Paul continued: "I appeal to you therefore, brothers, by the mercies of God, to present your bodies as a living sacrifice, holy and acceptable to God, which is your spiritual worship" (Romans 12:1). Note that Paul did not appeal to them by fear. In light of everything God has done for sinners in Christ, he appealed to the Roman Christians by God's great mercy. So also, God's great mercy becomes *your* primary motivation to love God and your neighbor. As St. John succinctly put it, "We love because He first loved us" (1 John 4:19).

Biblical ethics go hand in hand with God's grace. God is a loving God. Therefore, love Him and do what He says when He commands love for your neighbor. When all of your ethical striving falls short of God's glory, though, recall that God is gracious and merciful. He declares you righteous in Christ and so receives all the glory for your salvation. Biblical ethics are impossible without God's grace.

The *Secret* Teachings of Jesus

Shhhhh! It's a secret!

The public has an insatiable interest in secret teachings. Sales have skyrocketed for Rhonda Byrne's *The Secret*, both book and DVD. Christians still feel the shock waves from Dan Brown's international best seller *The Da Vinci Code*. It seems that another secret Gnostic gospel is printed afresh every Christmas and Easter. Marvin Meyer's *The Secret Teachings of Jesus: Four Gnostic Gospels* comes to mind. Among the more recent publications is the secret gospel bearing the provocative title *The Gospel of Judas*.

People seem fascinated with ancient secrets.

Do we Christians have secrets within our faith? Are there any secret teachings of Jesus? If so, what are they? What do they mean? What does the word *secret* mean in the New Testament? Mark 4 shows that Jesus did indeed have secret teachings. He taught secrets to bring about one of two results in His listeners: to withhold precious saving truths or to instruct those who are His.

The Parable of the Sower

Jesus was teaching a crowd, telling a parable in which a man sows seed (Mark 4:1–9). Some of the seed is snatched by birds, some falls on shallow soil, and some is chocked by thorns. None of these survive. Some seeds, however, take root. They grow and yield huge crops. Jesus concludes with these words: "He who has ears to hear, let him hear" (v. 9).

All this is simple enough. But when Jesus was alone with His inner circle, He told them, "To you has been given the secret of the kingdom of God, but for those outside everything is in parables, so that 'they may indeed see but not perceive, and may indeed hear but not understand, lest they should turn and be forgiven' " (Mark 4:11–12).

Why the secrecy? The quotation says that those outside may "*indeed* see but not perceive" and "may *indeed* hear but not understand." The outsiders saw and heard, all right, but they did not want to perceive and understand.

Think of the previous chapter in Mark. Jesus' opponents had watched Him carefully so that they might accuse Him. He was grieved at their hardness of heart. His enemies took the amazing step of becoming allies to destroy Him (Mark 3:1–6). They even accused Him of being demon possessed (Mark 3:22). They misunderstood Christ because they *wanted* to. It was for outsiders like these that Jesus hid his message in parables.

It's a *Mystery*

The Greek word translated "secret" in Mark 4:11 is *mysterion*, from which we get the word *mystery*. A *mysterion* is something normally beyond human comprehension and reason. Nonetheless, God has chosen to give a glimpse of it.

St. Paul wrote of "mysteries" hidden in ages past but now made known. Mysteries such as God's will (Ephesians 1:9) or Christ in you (Colossians 1:26–27) are revealed truths. Paul's statement to Timothy is like a beautiful small creed. "Great indeed, we confess, is the mystery of godliness: He was manifested in the flesh, vindicated by the Spirit, seen by angels, proclaimed among the nations, believed on in the world, taken up in glory" (1 Timothy 3:16).

When Jesus explained the parable of the sower, He revealed a secret. The irony is that the explanation raises more questions, questions that Jesus left unanswered: *Why* does God allow Satan to take some seed away? *Why* does God allow some seed to endure a while and then fall away? *Why* does God allow the deceitfulness and desires to choke the Word? The explanation that Christ gave is thus a *mystery in itself*. You get a piece of the truth—a glimpse, as it were. Yet Christ does not tell you everything.

Hardening

Evil itself is also mystery, a secret. Paul warned of "the mystery of lawlessness" (2 Thessalonians 2:7). Why were the scribes and Pharisees hardened? "Lest you be wise in your own conceits, I want you to understand this mystery, brothers: a partial hardening has come upon Israel" (Romans 11:25).

Some theologians call this teaching the doctrine of obduration, or stubbornness. Others simply refer to the reality as hardening the heart. This is when one repeatedly and stubbornly rejects God, resulting in God's rejection of that person. When people repeatedly harden their own hearts against God, He will eventually withdraw His grace and in this way *help* them harden their hearts.

If you fear that you have reached this point, the very fact that you are alarmed about the prospect shows that you have not reached it. Remember your Baptism, and trust your Savior! If you think you know someone else who has reached the point of no return, think again. "Man looks on the outward appearance, but the LORD looks on the heart" (1 Samuel 16:7). Our part is "speaking the truth in love" (Ephesians 4:15).

Getting One's Wish

A person gets to this point only if he persistently desires to. In Matthew, Jesus described hell as outer darkness (Matthew 8:12; 22:13; 25:30). Jesus spoke of those who "loved the darkness rather than the light" (John 3:19). In short, Jesus taught that some people want to be away from God. The Lord will eventually grant their wish to "depart" (Matthew 25:41). So Christ taught in parables that they "may indeed hear but not understand, lest they should turn and be forgiven" (Mark 4:12).

On the other hand, God's kingdom is primarily the presence of the biblical God. Some people spend their whole lives running from Him. In the end, they get exactly what they wish, eternity outside His presence.

So Why Teach Believers in Parables?

Instead of a demonstration of the truth in absolute terms, Christ taught in parables in part to give room for the Holy Spirit's work in the lives of believers. For "no one can say 'Jesus is Lord' except in the Holy Spirit" (1 Corinthians 12:3). As much as you may yearn for God to disclose Himself in some universally compelling way, for the time being God wants you to take Him at His Word by the power of His Spirit.

He also wants to encourage the faithful to know Him better, "to reach all the riches of full assurance of understanding and the knowledge of God's mystery, which is Christ" (Colossians 2:2). The mysteries, the secrets of God's kingdom, are not hidden *from* you. They are hidden *for* you. "To you has been given the secret of the kingdom of God" (Mark 4:11). The secret is Christ Himself, and you get to know Him through His Word. "Like newborn infants, long for the pure spiritual milk, that by it you may grown up to salvation—if indeed you have tasted that the Lord is good" (1 Peter 2:2–3).

The Best and Oldest Manuscripts Do Not Contain . . .

© RTimages, 2009 / Used under license from Shutterstock.com

Blogs Ablaze!

Many Internet blog sites are ablaze with claims and counterclaims in a verbal war over the Christian faith. The battleground is the public's collective mind-set. The weapon used by both Christian and anti-Christian alike is "textual criticism," the study of evidence for the reliability of ancient manuscripts. Once a discipline with relatively few devotees, textual criticism of the New Testament has now entered mainstream awareness, riding a wave of new publications. Books such as *Misquoting Jesus* and *The Incredible Shrinking Son of Man* are typical examples. Such books were written by scholars who themselves were formerly Christian. They help lay the groundwork for the new militant atheism.

Mark 16:9–20?

In evaluating and responding to these new publications, it is important to realize something: the problem here is unbelief, not the study of the evidence for manuscript reliability. New Testament manuscripts do differ from one another in places. The present article treats one of the most significant and famous differences between manuscripts. You may already have heard of this one: the various endings for the Gospel according to Mark.

Almost all contemporary translations of the New Testament insert a note after Mark 16:8. The English Standard Version provides several possible endings. In the field of textual criticism, these are called "variant readings." Entire books have been written about the variants at the end of Mark, such as the material designated as verses 9 through 20. (Other well-known variant readings include John 7:53–8:11; Acts 8:37; and 1 John 5:7–8.) We will see that if any of the "endings" of Mark are part of the book's original text, they teach nothing different from the rest of the Bible. On the other hand, if they are not part of what Mark wrote, this would not change our faith in the least.

What Do They Mean?

There are good, "Bible-believing" scholars who hold that none of the possible endings for Mark beyond verse 8 are Holy Scripture, for they do not believe that any of them were

© CPH

the book Mark wrote. Some of the oldest manuscripts contain nothing beyond Mark 16:8. Other manuscripts that include text in addition to verse 8 do so with markings such as asterisks.

Further, the "endings" contain some unusual choices of words. Some scholars go as far as to say that the theological content of the various "endings" conflicts with the rest of the Scriptures.

Let us then ask a question. If these variant readings are Scripture, what do they mean?

The Shorter Ending

Our first possible ending to Mark is a variant reading commonly called the shorter ending: "But they reported briefly to Peter and those with him all that they had been told. And after this, Jesus Himself sent out by means of them, from east to west, the sacred and imperishable proclamation of eternal salvation." If this passage was penned by Mark himself, there is nothing here that would alter the Christian faith. As we know from the other New Testament Gospels, the women *did* report and Jesus *did* send out His disciples to proclaim salvation from east to west. (See Luke 24:22–23 and Matthew 28:18–20.)

The Longer Ending

The more familiar ending is commonly called the traditional or longer ending. It contains Jesus' appearance to Mary Magdalene (Mark 16:9–11), His appearance to the two disciples (vv. 12–13), and finally His ascension (v. 19). These events are also found in John 20; Luke 24; and Acts 1. The familiar verse Mark 16:16 says that Baptism saves and unbelief condemns, as is also taught in 1 Peter 3:21 and John 3:18. Jesus predicts that His faithful will heal the sick, cast out demons, and pick up snakes, all of which occurred in the Acts of the Apostles. (See, for example, Acts 3:6–7; 5:14–16; 16:16–18; 28:1–6.)

The Even Longer Ending

Another manuscript version of Mark's Gospel has the longer traditional ending with an additional text in it following verse 14. In this material, Christ teaches that Satan's power has come to an end. This is also found in passages such as Mark 3:22–30; Luke 10:18; and 1 John 3:8.

All possible endings of Mark agree with the rest of the New Testament. They do not alter the Christian faith.

What If These Endings Are Not Scripture?

Some say that the Book of Mark cannot possibly end at 16:8. The verse reads, "They said nothing to anyone, for they were afraid." In the Greek, it ends with the word *for*. So some scholars argue that there simply *must* have been additional material following Mark 16:8. If none of the "endings" is part of Mark's original book, perhaps his material beyond verse 8 is now lost. Or maybe he was interrupted just as he was writing the word *for*.

Yet the word *for* can end a Greek sentence. Examples can be found in the Greek translation of the Old Testament, such as Genesis 18:15; 45:3; Isaiah 16:10; and Isaiah 29:11. In the New Testament, the Greek text of John 13:13 ends with the word *for*. Mark's Gospel could indeed end at verse 8.

No matter what Mark's ending was, we should not fail to notice: Christ is still arisen by Mark 16:8! A messenger assured the women at the tomb, "Do not be alarmed. You seek Jesus of Nazareth, who was crucified. He has risen; He is not here. See the place where they laid Him" (Mark 16:6). That report is in all ancient copies of Mark's Gospel.

The Importance of Textual Criticism

Textual criticism is a useful tool, even though some use it to disprove and discredit what God has said. If anything, careful textual study ought to enhance respect for the biblical text as text. Critics often doubt because they *want* to doubt. We need to learn something about these issues, because textual criticism is turning into a major battleground, with souls at stake.

The ending of Mark stands out as one of a few instances in which a relatively lengthy section of text, several verses, comes into question. Yet, as noted above, the variant readings do not affect the doctrinal content of the New Testament. God not only wrote the Scriptures through the apostles and prophets, but He also used the work of faithful scribes down through the centuries to preserve the biblical text to this day. All of this is to bring you forgiveness and life in Jesus Christ!